AF700298

Illustrated by

Jeff Pace

Copyright © 1995
Behavioral Science Center, Inc., Publications

All rights reserved.
No part of this book may be used or reproduced in any manner without written permission, except for brief quotations embodied in reviews or critical articles.

Cover illustration is a digital photocomposition of illustrations by Max Elbo and Jeff Pace

For more information, write:

Ann Adams
Silver Boat Productions
393 Timberlake Ln. • Eureka Springs, AR 72631
501-253-6795 ajn@arkansas.net

Editor-in-Chief: William C. Wester, II, Ed.D.
Manuscript Editor: Shoshana D. LeVine, Ed.D.

First Printing, October, 1994

Printed in the United States of America

Library of Congress Catalog Card Number 94-072355

ISBN 0-938837-17-6

To: Alison, for your friendship, assistance and support

For: Inner Dragons, who provide the strength for survival and healing journeys

For: Those of us who continue to struggle with our own dragons. May the lessons in these adventures transform us into strong, secure and loving beings.

For: Pappa Manny

Part I

"Tell me again, Father, the story of the little girl, the lady in blue light, the children, and the dragon." And, "Yes," he said, as he began to get more and more excited, "of the swan and the silver boat."

Two seagulls were flying high and white against a blue sky. They often flew this way together. The larger gull enjoyed telling his son stories over and over again. Because the stories were so lifelike, the young gull often felt himself to be right there in the midst of the action as the plot unfolded. Today, the father had planned something exciting for his son. Rather than retell the story of the little girl, the gull wanted to continue this story in a very special and surprising way. He signaled for his son to follow. The son nodded.

From their place high in the sky, the older gull began drifting downward in slow circles. The younger gull followed, feeling his body and mind becoming very relaxed. The circling seemed to last forever, but in fact took only a few seconds. A blue light traced the path of their circles.

Once there was a little girl...
Kit

Soon the gulls could see the ocean spread out beneath them. Just like the circling, the ocean seemed to go on forever. As they continued to spiral downward, the older gull began speaking.

"The little girl, her hair sparkling in the sun, stepped into the boat," said the father. Upon hearing the first few words of the story, the young gull magically saw a small silver boat in the sea. In it was the little girl. The gentle swan swam forward, pulling the tiny vessel.

"The little girl was happy but also a bit overwhelmed by her trip through the forest," said the father gull very quietly, not wanting to distract his son from what he was seeing. "As she heard waves splashing softly against the sides of the tiny vessel, the little girl nestled in satin pillows which lined the floor of the boat. Sunlight kept her warm as she drifted off to sleep."

"Her dreams were of all that had happened in the forest and at the seaside. The lady in blue light floated once again in the child's mind. The little girl smiled and at the same time felt the soft pillow upon which her cheek rested.

"The swan, pleased with itself for being part of this important journey, steadily moved through the calm water. Every so often the swan would turn its long graceful neck so that it could gaze upon the sleeping child. Spreading open one of its wings, the swan would for a few moments shade the little girl from the sun. In some mysterious way, the swan seemed to share her dreams.

"While most of her dreams were pleasant, the little girl couldn't keep the dragon from pushing his way into them. Her drifting dreams would come to a halt as the dragon once again thundered on the path, turning around and around in anger and confusion. In her sleep, the little girl felt the dragon's anger and confusion as if it were her own. In the boat she turned restlessly and repositioned herself, seeking some comfort in the pillows. The swan looked back at her with concern."

The young gull also became restless. "I thought she was finished with the dragon," he said. "I want to hear about the little girl and her journey."

"Ah," said the father gull. "It is sad and dangerous to ignore dragons or even to pretend that they are not a part of all journeys, even your own. What do you think happened to the dragon?"

Recalling the story once again, the young gull said, "The dragon dizzily slurked away, while the little girl and the children ran to the sea."

"That is correct," said the father gull. "But what about the dragon?"

"Oh," said the younger gull, realizing that he was going to hear about the dragon whether he wanted to or not. "I never really thought any more about the dragon. What did happen to him?"

"I'll tell you. No, better still, I'll show you," said the father gull, "but first we'll have to fly back in time." As he said this, the father gull made another large arc in the sky. Together they swirled 'round and 'round through the air. The younger gull found himself once again getting caught up in circles and in blue light. Both gulls soon found themselves at the edge of the sea next to the forest.

"Look, Father," said the younger gull. "We *are* back in time! There's the little girl and the children playing and splashing in the water. They don't even know yet about the swan and the silver boat."

The gulls flew on. As they flew deeper into the forest and further back in time, the adventurers spied the dragon. The younger gull dropped back a bit and peaked out from behind his father's wing. The dragon, who had just been told off by the children, was dizzily slurking away and vowing never again to fool with children.

"But his vows never lasted," continued the father gull. "So deep were his anger, hurt, and need for revenge that the second he started rebuilding his strength, the dragon started plotting his revenge."

"Curses and double curses!" said the dragon, as he thumped his giant clawed foot on the ground so forcefully that the trees in the forest began to quiver. "I'll get even over and over again." The dragon had gotten even so many times with so many different animals, children, and, yes, even with the very forest itself. And over and over again, in all his strength, the dragon stood alone.

He began thundering through the forest swatting at trees for what seemed like hours. His mind swarmed with memories — stinging memories — of having been shamed and hurt over and over, of dark objects looming over him. Lashing out at the trees seemed to make the memories go away. And over and over again, in all his strength, the dragon stood alone.

As he tore the trees from the ground one after another, the beast convinced himself that the trees deserved this treatment. He always felt himself to be the one wronged, even when he had started the trouble. The dragon shook with emotion. He took in a deep breath, then an even deeper breath. In all his strength, the dragon stood alone, but this time he found himself to be very lonely.

As the dragon exhaled, mighty flames tore from his nose and mouth. At the same time, the dragon unexpectedly slumped to the ground. It wasn't for lack of strength or might. It was sadness which weighted him so. Thoughts of all his unhappy victories clamored in his head. Large tears ran down his face and sizzled, turning to steam as they met the heat of his once fiery nostrils. He sobbed, "I'm tired of trying to get even. I don't even know why I'm so angry. Something has to change."

It was then that he first noticed a spark of blue light on the tip of one of his massive wings. The dragon stretched his long neck while blinking the tears from his eyes to get a closer look. He lifted the wing to the sky. The dragon curiously watched the point of light as it moved slowly — first tracing the outline of his wing — and then as it spread through his entire body. He felt a warm tingle.

Strangely enough, the dragon knew to breathe deeply and allow his mind to go within. As his mind travelled deeply, the dragon, now completely covered in blue light, could hear the sounds of the children laughing and playing in the water. Somehow he knew that soon the little girl would be part of an adventure which would take her across the sea to a warm and sunny land. As his mind went even deeper, he said to himself, "I wish I could go, too, but who would want a dragon in a warm and sunny land?"

It was then that the dragon heard a soft voice saying to him, "You must think of what you want rather that what you fear." He thought of fun and laughter and of not being alone.

As if in a dream, the dragon felt his mighty wings, which were still tingling with blue light, spread widely. He didn't resist. The dragon's long neck lifted, and then his body. He was flying!

"How strange this is," said the dragon out loud as he began to fly. He heard the wind rushing past him as he wound in circles through the air in the direction of the sea. He felt different, as if the mere desire to change in some way had started something magical.

Like most dragons, he'd never really enjoyed flying. But this was different. "I feel different. My body feels so light. I could fly forever." As he spun through the air, the dragon briefly saw the group of children playing in the water. They were having so much fun splashing and singing that they didn't even see or hear him.

The giant animal awakened from his dreamlike state to find himself gently touching down at the water's edge. As he looked at his reflection in the water, he couldn't believe his eyes. "The neck is long, but is it mine? My wings are so different!" said the dragon in a whisper. Instead of a massive dragon, the mirror of the water showed him to be a lovely white swan.

He stared in disbelief at the reflection. "This can't be me," he said to himself as he turned to find the swan. Instead of a swan, there stood next to him the lady in blue light.

"Yes," she said, "the reflection is yours. You, too, are part of this journey. There is much which you and the little girl need to learn about anger and strength, about accepting yourselves and each other."

Then, smiling, the lady handed him a ribbon which was attached to a silver boat. Holding onto the ribbon, the white swan waited quietly at the water's edge for the little girl.

Part II

"My goodness, Father," said the young gull who seemed himself to be awakening from a dream. "Was the swan really the dragon all along? What will happen to the little girl now? Is she safe? Is the swan a swan or is it that dangerous dragon? Why did the dragon change into a swan? Has the dragon really changed?"

The father gull laughed. He enjoyed watching his son become so caught up in stories. "You'll have to wait and see," said the father, once again in a quiet voice which was almost a whisper. As the father spoke, the scene on the ocean reappeared to the young gull. The swan, the silver boat and the little girl moved steadily in the immense sea.

The little girl stirred from her sleep. Thoughts raced through her head: thoughts of her dreams, of the lady in blue light, of the dragon, his anger and frustration. She smiled at the swan. The swan looked at her. There seemed to be an understanding between them, but neither was sure what it all meant.

Then, looking all around, the little girl smiled again, stood up and stretched her arms to the sky. The boat rocked a bit. She purposely swayed, a playful move which allowed her to gain control of the rocking and to hold her balance. The swan turned to look at her, his blue eyes shining in the sun. She waved a hand. As she sat down, the little girl thought to herself, "I've seen blue eyes like those before."

It was a glorious day. White puffy clouds seemed to be playing games of hide and seek in the breezes which stirred high above. The squawking of two seagulls alerted the little girl and the swan to a spectacle off in the distance. As they looked, each could see dolphins gracefully arching through the air: first, one at a time, then in twos, and then in threes. The dolphins made clicking noises and sang high-pitched songs. Eyeing the travelers, the chuckling sea creatures sent sonar waves toward the silver boat.

The sonar spun through the water in silver streaks which transformed into blue light as it bounced off the travelers. The returning sonar met the now approaching dolphins with news about the travelers. The dolphins gleefully sped toward the little boat, sending mind messages ahead of them to the little girl and the swan.

"Greetings from the sea," sang the messages. "We are here to play with you. We are your next guides. Before you continue on your way, you will learn lightness of heart. Now it is time for fun!"

The dolphins seemed to be chasing their own messages. Right in the midst of the message, three dolphins shot up from deep beneath the water and flew high over the travelers. Each shiny body sprinkled silvery showers of light upon the swan, the little girl, and the silver boat.

The little girl, who had only dreamed of such experiences, screamed with delight. The swan, on the other hand, watched cautiously as his eyes became larger and larger.

Sensing the swan's hesitancy to join in the fun, the dolphins, clicking and laughing, swam 'round and 'round him. The swan, who was not accustomed to fun, felt awkward at first, but as the air became thick with songs and glee, he, too, began smiling broadly and joined in the festivities by flying in and out of the dancing and soaring dolphins.

During one leap, a dolphin flew over the boat, sweeping the little girl onto its back. Through the sea they sailed, as she held onto its dorsal fin. Even though she began to become fearful of this bold adventure, the child held on and allowed herself to trust the dolphin. The swan flew along, bewildered by it all, even by the two seagulls who flew next to him.

The little girl was about to burst with happiness. "I didn't know that I could feel this way," she shrieked. Much to her surprise, she sounded just like the dolphin. At that second her eyes mingled with the blue eyes of the swan who was next to her. Both knew that they, along with the dolphins, had been thinking the same thoughts and enjoying the same day.

The merriment went on for hours. Before leaving, the dolphins once again splashed trillions of silver streaks of light upon the travelers. In the midst of the splashing, the swan and the little girl heard:

"Remember these experiences whenever you wish. . . We will play with you, in your mind or in the sea. As you play with us, this joy and confidence will return to you."

"Watch me, Father!" said the young seagull as he imitated the flights of the dolphins. He even tried to click and whistle, most unusual sounds for a seagull.

"I love this new story! Flying with the dolphins was stupendous!" He suddenly halted. "Were we really there?" asked the young gull as he nearly lost the balance of his flight.

Knowing that his father was not going to answer most of his questions, the son continued without even waiting for answers.

"What happens next? Do they all get to live happily ever after yet?" clicked the son as he imagined sprinkling silver light from his dolphin arch. He was so proud of himself for having learned new sounds and moves.

The father gull smiled and continued in the familiar quiet voice, "After the dolphins left, the little girl and the swan recalled over and over again their gleeful experiences. They were both amazed by the mind communication of the dolphins, and by the fact that their own thoughts seemed to mingle one with the other. Both looked forward to more encounters with the dolphins, either in the sea or in their minds.

"The little girl, wringing out sections of her dress, and still tasting the saltiness of the water upon her lips, looked to the sky, to puffy clouds. Off to the left she noticed that some of the lighter clouds were being replaced by heavier ones."

"Why is it getting so dark?" wondered the little girl as one particularly large cloud moved between her and the sun. As the sky darkened, the light breezes seemed to become cooler and heavier. The little girl's hair blew in the wind. With a frightened gesture she brushed her hair from her eyes. The once bright and friendly sea was turning into a brownish grey color. Larger waves began splashing against the boat.

Even though he began to struggle with the swelling waves, the swan was determined to keep swimming. He swam with all of his strength, but moved forward very slowly. The tiny boat began to toss around, almost toppling over. As the winds became wilder, the swan tugged with all its might, but failed to advance the boat. At times the force of the waves and the tossing boat dragged the swan sideways and backwards.

The little girl noticed her hands turning white as she clutched at the sides of the tiny boat. Her fear grew along with every wave. "I was silly to believe that anything good could happen to me," she cried. "This feels like a trick."

The swan looked back at her. At that moment he glared with cold blue eyes. He began thinking, "I was foolish to believe that anything good could happen to me. Now I have given up all of my strength. I'm no use to myself or anyone," he cried in frustration.

The little girl said to herself, "Where have I seen those eyes before?" Her fear heightened. Just then a large wave splashed against the boat, dumping water into her tiny vessel. She desperately began trying to empty water from the boat with one small hand, while holding on with the other. Her feet slipped around in the bottom of the boat.

When she looked up again, she saw the beautiful swan twist and thrash in the turbulent water. He, too, became more and more fearful, then very angry. He thought of abandoning the little girl and flying to safety, but deep in his heart, this is not what he wanted to do.

He took a deep breath, closed his eyes briefly, and wished for his strength. As he exhaled, the swan felt his wings and legs growing. His neck extended high above his body, which began to take up more and more space in the water. The silver boat and the little girl looked very small to him now.

The little girl watched this transformation in utter amazement. For a moment she seemed to forget about the storm.

"It was a trick!" she panicked. "All along you were the dragon!"

For a second the winds seemed to calm; but out of the corner of her eye, the little girl could see something very tall and broad in the distance. She swung her head around. A roaring wave was growing and moving closer to the boat by the second. "I am lost!" cried the little girl to the dragon. Their eyes connected.

In a flash, both the little girl and the dragon closed their eyes and quickly thought of the dolphins and the blue light. The dragon stretched one of his mighty closed wings behind him to rest at the side of the boat. As the wave began to break over its top, the dragon opened his wing like a giant fan, sheltering the tiny boat and the little girl.

The thundering wave crashed against him, and then, as if changing its mind, tamely curled off of the wing spread by the dragon. The little girl was safe. Then, with wings spread behind him to each side of the boat, the dragon calmly swam through the raging sea, sheltering the silver boat.

The little girl was in a state of wonder and dismay. "How can this be?" she exclaimed. It was then that she noticed the outline of blue light around the wings and the entire body of the dragon. Somehow, once again she felt safe, even with the dragon.

As the storm calmed, dolphins reappeared, clapping their flippers in the air and creating rainbows in sprays of water and light. They beamed blessings and scores of sacred messages. The dragon came to understand that in order to become nicer, he didn't have to give up his strength. The little girl just leaned back, and together with the dragon, held these events in her heart.

Each became more and more familiar with the other, trading memories and feelings without even talking. They grew closer and closer: the dragon with the beautiful softness of the little girl, and the child with the strength of the dragon. Both the dragon and the little girl watched with amusement as two sea gulls, an older and younger, circled 'round and 'round them. On this glorious day, the seagulls seemed to be celebrating life itself.

About the Author

ANN ADAMS, R.N.P., M.N.Sc.

Born in New Orleans, Louisiana, Ms. Adams is a Registered Nurse Practitioner in private practice in Eureka Springs, Arkansas. She is also employed at St. John's Adolescent Treatment Center in Springfield, Missouri. She has a Masters Degree in Mental Health Nursing from the University of Arkansas for the Medical Sciences.

In addition to **The Silver Boat**, Ms. Adams has authored chapters in **Mental Health-Psychiatric Nursing**, and **Clinical Manual of Psychiatric Nursing**, and has written *"Internal Self Helpers of Persons with Multiple Personality Disorder," an* article for the **Journal of Dissociation**. She has presented papers at the annual conference of the International Society for the Study of Multiple Personality and Dissociation (1987, 1988, 1989 and 1990). After publication of The Silver Boat, she was invited to the Menninger Clinic (1992) as a Visiting Professor for two days of lectures & consultations and presented at the VOICES conference, 1993.

Ms. Adams loves the ocean and has spent time swimming for hours at a time with a pod of 47 wild dolphins in Hawaii.

About the Artist

JEFF PACE

Jeff lives with his wife, Holly, and their two cats, Boo and Romeo in Fayetteville, Arkansas.